ABANDONED EASTERN KENTUCKY

JAY FARRELL

AMERICA THROUGH TIME®
ADDING COLOR TO AMERICAN HISTORY

America Through Time is an imprint of Fonthill Media LLC
www.through-time.com
office@through-time.com

Published by Arcadia Publishing by arrangement with Fonthill Media LLC
For all general information, please contact Arcadia Publishing:
Telephone: 843-853-2070
Fax: 843-853-0044
E-mail: sales@arcadiapublishing.com
For customer service and orders:
Toll-Free 1-888-313-2665

www.arcadiapublishing.com

First published 2020

ISBN 978-1-63499-272-5

Typeset in Trade Gothic 10pt on 15pt
Printed and bound in England

CONTENTS

ABOUT THE AUTHOR

JAY FARRELL is a Nashville, Tennessee, based photographer who loves photographing abandoned structures. He has a passion for utilizing his camera to share the unique, distressed beauty of abandoned homes and structures that most of the world has forgotten. Sharing his adventures with the public through authorship and blogging inspires him as much as the adventures themselves.

INTRODUCTION

The "life after people" feel to abandoned buildings, complete with rotted and caving floors, old contents of yesteryear left behind, and the overall entropy and distress are what fuels my inspiration. There's a freedom (and a danger) of exploring the back road to seek these abandoned treasures. These structures tell a story. The goal for my abandoned building photos is to tell their stories, and be their voice after they've been forgotten, sometimes for generations. An unlikely artistic subject often makes the most powerful art, not for its worldly beauty, but the beauty and character that only abandoned building enthusiasts understand.

This book features the work from my travels and adventures in various locations in Eastern Kentucky. You'll enjoy my first trip through the Northeast Kentucky Appalachian foothills, with full autumnal colors, and quaint blighted countryside structures. My next excursions take you through my journeys throughout a variety of Southeastern Kentucky locations in the old coal mining towns and countryside. This book features a founder's historic mansion, old coal company store, bone-chilling hallways of a former company town high school, and so much more. As I make footsteps into the forgotten, I discover structures surrounded by fallen materials and overgrowth, all suffering the effects of time.

Eastern Kentucky is a special place with rich history, industry, beautiful mountains, valleys, waterways, private hollers, and misty mountaintops on overcast days. Locals know when outsiders lurk in their alert and closely-knit communities. My experience was favorable; as I spoke with the natives and showed interest in the area, I found them to be very kind, genuine, and hospitable. Eastern Kentuckians are known for that hospitality and transparency. However, strangers who take the wrong approach or are perceived as a threat could find themselves in trouble.

In this book, I take you up close and personal to places unknown to most, far deeper than the roadside view would provide. You will experience the true feel of Eastern Kentucky and coal country through my lens. I hope you enjoy it!

Take only pictures, leave only footprints. [*Illustration by Kelly J. King*]

1

RAMBLING AROUND ROWAN COUNTY

After making an author appearance outside of Louisville, I traveled to Rowan County in Northeastern Kentucky to do some exploring. The morning I began my adventure was a day made for exploring, with chilly, misty, overcast conditions. The autumnal colors in late October were a picturesque garnish to the Appalachian landscape while navigating the narrow roads through mountains and valleys. My excursion throughout Rowan County was made up of several random stops, and expanded into Carter and Elliott Counties on different occasions.

My first stop was in a tiny community originally called "Smile," which was later renamed to "Big Brushy." Looks were deceiving, as far as the identity of the two neighboring buildings; thankfully, the Rowan County historian cleared the mystery up for me. Photo captions will fill you in on the details.

After several hours of exploring, I found myself back in a different part of Rowan County. I stopped at a small general store to grab some lunch and bump elbows with a couple of friendly locals. This was a nice local experience, and the lady who served me lunch even told me about an old vacant farmhouse several miles away.

I thought this was an old one-room schoolhouse, but it was originally Smile Church, then Big Brushy Church. It was named after the community both times.

This was years after the last hanging of the greens.

The back view of the old crumbling church.

Now you get an inside view, including an old pew.

Above: That bare light bulb over the sparse pulpit area looks so grim in its current state.

Left: This electric service is *circa* 1940s, according to an electrician I know. I'd hazard a guess that lights and maybe a heater were the only things electric in this old church. Perhaps there was a piano, and definitely an outhouse, at one time.

This old Fryman's Chapel building used to be Smile School, then Big Brushy School. So, the building everyone thinks was a schoolhouse was a church, and vice versa.

The picnic grove is looking a bit sad these days.

On the next leg of my journey, I stumbled upon this large house sitting in the weeds and trees, displaying full autumn colors.

The outside was far more interesting than the inside, so I will spare you the 1970s woodgrain walls, red carpet, and lack of contents inside.

Right: Speaking of walls, this photo will soon be hanging on my own walls.

Below: This angle more accurately shows how huge this house really is, and the level of distress.

Left: The basement door didn't lead to any treasures, except itself.

Below: On a narrow backroad with nothing around, sat this random shanty house that begged for my exploration.

The front was overgrown, and the porch was badly rotted. The back was not much different.

After nearly falling through the front porch floor, I got inside to see some dated furniture, as well as other weathered remnants.

You've traveled a long way to come see me. May I fix you a plate or pour you a cup of tea? At one time, that conversation may have happened in this exact spot. Maybe not recently, however.

Close the door behind you. Were you raised in a barn?

After exploring Carter County, I ended up back in a different part of Rowan County, which was all the same to me. After enjoying lunch at a small community general store, I followed the lead the storekeeper provided, several miles away. I don't always socialize on these missions; however, she found what I do interesting.

This water well was behind this falling farmhouse, and I would bet that water was cold even in the dog days of summer.

Above left: The only access to this house was to cross a small creek to get to the field. This rickety back porch was my best access inside the house, but we take what we can get in this game. The front door had a cement block tied to the front door so that it wouldn't fly open in the wind.

Above right: Farm related items were stored in the house, so besides being on the business end of my lens, it still serves a purpose.

Layers of color, wallpaper, board, and other fallen materials all came together in this photo for the greater good.

That wallpaper was not manufactured, but developed over time. We'll call it "custom mold." Literally.

I wonder what the story is with all the pine straw all over the floors? Maybe to cushion one's fall through the floor? Thoughtful.

A climb up the stairs revealed a dormer room with a sick green shag carpet. I'm glad I made the trek.

This is the aforementioned security system for the front door.

I couldn't tell you the last I saw an International Harvester Travelall. There was one sitting off the road near the previous farmhouse. They were manufactured between 1953 and 1975. Scouts and Travelalls were not known for body integrity and often rusted prematurely, making this an unusual find.

This old International didn't achieve this level of character and distress overnight. This was likely decades in the making.

This particular Travelall was likely an early 1970s model. There were few distinguishing differences in the fourth and final generation design, spanning from 1969 to 1975.

2

PLUMBING PROBLEMS

On different occasions throughout the long day of exploring, I crossed paths with different counties, and unknowingly ended up in different parts of the same ones again. The first thing that sticks out in my mind about Carter County was seeing a used car lot called "Lying Lee's." I knew that I was in a good place for exploring when I saw that. I appreciated the humor and play on a stereotype of that type of business. Lee is probably well known in the community and the catchy name obviously works for him.

The first stop was a rather random and unusual one. My first observation was a burnt shell of a building, which apparently was a plumbing supply store. Next to it, buried in tall brush, was a dilapidated old early 1900s-era house that was loaded with old plumbing parts itself. After exploring there, and later in the day landing in a different part of the county, I stopped for gas and met a family in a chance encounter who told me about an old schoolhouse. They even graciously offered to lead me to it.

After seeing the plumbing supplies sign on the side of the adjacent house, with an arrow pointing to this burnt shell of a building, I had my answer as to what this was.

I almost couldn't see this hidden roadside gem with all the overgrowth surrounding it.

Right: I could read that plumbing supplies sign just fine, but that little orange "No Trespassing" sign I couldn't quite distinguish at the time.

Below: Well, I suppose it goes without saying that the side entrance isn't the best way in.

I didn't expect to see plumbing parts inside the house, but they were plentiful.

Hey fella, couldn't you wait until we're open on Monday before entering our store? Never mind, that train left the station years ago. Carry on.

This very old mid-century suitcase was one of the very few personal belongings left behind

As I squeezed through the brush on my way out, a lady across the road looked at me. I waved, and she saw my camera and said, "Oh you're just taking photos? Knock yourself out, you don't look like a crackhead. I don't own it anyhow." It's nice to know I have your blessing and that I don't look like a crackhead. Life is good.

This is the schoolhouse that the nice local family directed me to. It sits on property that since has been built on by the family who purchased the land. It was an active one-room schoolhouse until the mid-1960s, later used as an apartment until its condition deteriorated too much.

The color alone made me almost go black and white. But it's too ugly to hide. I wouldn't even know how to describe that color, but the schoolhouse was a charming piece of history.

3

THE COMMUNITY GROCER

On a frosty morning through the Eastern Kentucky mountains, I traveled through the hills and valleys of Knox and Bell Counties, subsequently finding some intriguing roadside surprises. The roadside discovery that demanded the most effort to hunt down history was the old Paul Green Grocery. With the help of friendly locals, I was able to locate Danny Green, whose father, Paul Green, was the community grocer. The original location was a half mile away from the current defunct store, in the Blackmont community of Bell County, operating from 1964-1971. In 1971, the store relocated to the location pictured, in the community known as Hulen, formerly Alva. Previously, the building housed both a small store and roller-skating rink.

The community store sold groceries, animal feed, and a small selection of general household goods and children's toys. Like many Eastern Kentucky communities, most were single-income coal miner families, sometimes struggling to make ends meet. Like many small-town general stores of bygone eras, Mr. Green extended credit to many local families through weekly or monthly tabs. Unfortunately, good deeds don't always go unpunished, and some families did not repay their debt to the store. Mr. Green refused to let anyone in his community go hungry—that's just who he was.

Mr. Green also butchered deer, cattle, and hogs for his customers for a very affordable price, operating out of a back room in the store. The pocket change gave him something for his time and covered the wrapping paper. The true reward was using his skills to serve the community, who often gave him some of the meat to help feed his own family.

Danny remembers his father sharing how he and his brother would collect coal that fell off the trains in onion sacks and sell it to the community. The boys used that money to catch a bus into Harlan and see a movie. The entrepreneur spirit began at an early age, and a community legacy was born. Mr. Green retired and closed the store in 2000, and is still remembered locally.

PAUL GREEN GROCERY
Coca-Cola
Coca-Cola

Oh the irony. Thank you for telling me, I never would have guessed! I'm told this was the "Puff and Stuff," a former greasy spoon type of restaurant. It was located right at the Bell and Harlan County line, and used to produce its share of grease smoke out of the smokestack. Healthy, no, but delicious, yes.

Opposite above: This location of Paul Green Grocery operated from 1971-2000. I knew that the history and overall impact on the community was richer than I could have imagined. I appreciated Danny's information, as the story is now more complete.

Opposite below: This cabin is likely from the Civil War era, and was definitely worth a closer look. It appears there have been window upgrades to completely dry the house in. There was nothing else surrounding the cabin on a large piece of otherwise empty land. I cannot recall if it was in Knox or Bell County, though very near the county line.

4

THE WHITTLER

On days when the sun shines and hits the mountaintops, it doesn't mean there aren't shadows in the valleys, except when sun is highest. To quote a Darrell Scott song, "You'll Never Leave Harlan Alive": "Where the sun comes up about ten in the morning, and the sun goes down about three in the day."

Randomly, I discovered the small community of Wallins Creek in Harlan County. The city was established in 1925 by Wallins Creek Coal Corporation. Once a thriving coal community is now an unincorporated city with no mayor and an approximate population of 150. In Wallins Creek, and Eastern Kentucky in general, many of the coal mining companies have ceased or decreased operations since their heyday, leaving coal families to fend for themselves.

It was common in the peak coal era for coal companies to create their own proprietary currency to pay their employees with, supplement, and/or provide payday advances, known as scrip. Scrip was only redeemable at their company store, and also helped the store by limiting cash on hand. Mining companies ran the towns, establishing their own banks, schools, company stores, housing for workers, and even churches. The company retained control and profit, forcing employee loyalty at any cost. To quote Tennessee Ernie Ford, "Another day older and deeper in debt, Saint Peter don't call me cause I can't go. I owe my soul to the company store."

As I entered the valley, I stopped to photograph three building shells. Curious about their history, I approached an older gentleman in work clothing sitting in front of a tiny community general store/used tire shop, whittling a small piece of wood. I never dreamt I'd experience a stereotypical Hollywood scene like this in real life. The man informed me that the small cobblestone building behind us was the old jailhouse and city hall. I was able to connect with an area historian to find out details on the other buildings. Despite flooding on several occasions and local industry declining, the small Cumberland River Valley community remains proud and tightly knit.

This is the former home of Howard Dry Cleaners. The shop oporated on the lower level, and the couple lived in an upstairs apartment. The historian also thought that local Masons and Oddfellows used a room on the upstairs level to hold meetings. In the late 1960s, the building was used as a welding/vocational school.

What was once a pharmacy and upstairs apartment is now a shell used to house a few used automobile parts.

Random trivia : A pharmacy/drug store in England is often referred to as "the chemist." The chemist left the building in the 1970s.

The Wallins Jailhouse and city hall was built in the 1920s by Italian stone masons using native stone. There were two jail cells that had no plumbing or electricity, and metal tray bunk beds. From what I learned, the blankets didn't go across the road to the cleaners often enough.

The sign once said “Wallins City Hall.”

Now choked by brush and only crumbling ruins remaining, I documented history in its last stages of life.

Above left: I'm assuming the toilet was for city hall, not the jails. The jail doors still remained, with "Do Not Enter" spray painted on both doors.

Above right: The cells were as dark as a cave; however, the light peeked its way in through the walls and ceilings. Even traffic violations were subject to jail time.

Right: The jail cell doors and stonework still stood strong. The building has been vacant since the early 1970s.

Below: I made my way to the backroads that took me into Leslie County, and along the way, I came across this roadside gem, Smith Auto Parts. A local lady told me the business closed ten years before my visit. The new owners bought the building for the parts inventory, and had not yet done anything with the building.

Nature is claiming its rightful spot, but memories don't die easily.

Although it was an auto parts store, the shop also did machine work, towing, and automobile and radiator repairs.

I liked the simple but interesting juxtaposition of the folding metal chair with icicles formed on it, sitting alongside a tiny abandoned town utility building.

5

PIKEVILLE PONTIAC PARTS

As this exploring day was winding down, I navigated through the valleys and mountains of Pike County, which neighbors Williamson, West Virginia. My two final stops for the day were very different, but nonetheless a great compliment to one another. From the road, I spotted a house that was partially standing, and another wing was completely collapsed. It was an optical illusion at first, as I couldn't distinguish whether the house had a connected add-on, or if there were different structures altogether. Trudging through thick straw-like grass and prickly thorn bushes, I finally reached the point of entry of the part of the house that actually had an inside to explore.

On the corner of the two-lane blacktop I was traveling, and a randomly selected backroad, sat a garage-like structure (that someone may have also lived in) belching out copious amounts of smoke from the smokestack chimney. Behind it, tucked away from the backroad, sat a derelict old farmhouse strewn with litter, dozens of immobilized old cars and trucks, and a plethora of automobile parts. It was important to be as discreet as possible and avoid potential hostility from the garage neighbors nearby.

The door wasn't open, but it wasn't locked, either. It was safe to say no one was home, so in I went. Which was fun, but a questionable decision. Not the first questionable decision I made.

This door had a hasp and lock on it. The part that wasn't accessible anyhow. Go figure.

I still don't know if this was an attached or detached structure—originally anyhow. We know what it is now.

What were you expecting? This? Me too.

I suppose this is the gateway to the crumbling wing.

The dishwashing liquid seems useless without running water, but it was a nice thought. Cleanliness is important, lest we forget.

Now we move to the house/automobile salvage yard.

Sometimes all you need are old Pontiac hubcaps. These folks may or may not sell them to you.

Pictured here is an early to mid-1970s Ford pickup truck, which may never move from this spot again.

The house was locked up; however, it wouldn't surprise me if it was also loaded with old car parts.

Now THIS is a classic tow truck of a bygone era. I'm sure it could tell many stories.

Front angle of mid-1960s Ford tow truck.

Above: Nothing here is eating any hay. If anyone still oversees these forgotten Detroit steel gems, despite the disheveled look of the complex, I bet they know where everything is.

Right: This is a heavy steel filing and storage cabinet. The Mon Ark sticker was a boat company from 1959-2008.

6

HAULING COAL

The Sunday morning sun made its presence in the hollers of Pike County where my journey continued. On a gravel road leading to a hilltop, I noticed some old mining equipment that looked like it had been out of service for a time. All that remained at the bottom of the mine was a conveyor belt to load the coal trucks that raced up and down the mountain roads, with little chance of stopping for a lane overlapping motorist. There are two kinds of coal mining. In deep mines, miners go into the mountain and underground and chip away the coal, and use train cars to transport coal. These mines could be miles deep. Strip mining is scraping coal off the mountaintop itself.

Neither kind of mining is nearly as prevalent in Eastern Kentucky anymore for many reasons, which has hurt the local economy. Awareness of black lung, environmental hazards, mine safety (including mines collapsing and miners dying), political influence, and other factors turned many thriving coal communities into near ghost towns. A local man told me that many miners had no other marketable skills that the area could support. Some had limited education and limited financial resources, making it difficult for those families to relocate elsewhere for other opportunities.

Making my journey towards Martin County, on a rural backroad with plenty of hills and curves, I decided to tune into local radio to see what was available for a change of pace. Most of the radio stations either had religious programming/preaching, bluegrass, or gospel music. There are many things that Eastern Kentuckians are serious about, faith being one of them. Stay tuned for more on that topic—it gets entertaining.

The backroad I was traveling ran somewhat parallel to the Tug Fork River, with West Virginia on the other side of the river. I approached Warfield and noticed an overgrown railroad bridge going across the Tug River into Kermit, West Virginia. This railroad bridge was used to transport coal and lumber to and from West Virginia, when the Himlerville Coal Company operated.

The mine entrance seldom had a quiet moment in its heyday. Now it sits with the beaten paths overgrown, and remaining equipment rusting away. In complete silence.

The old Gwenco mine in Pike County once kept the coal trucks screaming up and down the Eastern Kentucky roads. This conveyor was used to load coal into delivery trucks.

I'm guessing this was the material staging area.

"Supply Room, no trespassing." I did anyway, but nothing was in it.

You didn't think this contraption ran on batteries, did you?

Left: Now overgrown and out of service, this railroad trestle was once the bridge between states and communities, keeping the goods coming and going.

Below: The sun and shadows give the bridge and pillars a haunting presence, and a vast contrast of the relevance it had when business was booming.

7

HIMLERVILLE MANSION

In 1909, Hungarian immigrant Martin Himler made his journey to America in search of a better opportunity, with just pennies in his pockets. With previous experience working in Hungarian coal mines, Himler worked in Pennsylvania, Virginia, and West Virginia coal mines. Himler's entrepreneur spirit came to life when he became a successful newspaper editor with his own coal miners' publication written in both Hungarian and English. In 1919, Himler started the Himler Coal Company in what became known as Himlerville, Kentucky (now known as Beauty, Kentucky).

This was the first co-op coal mine, as he recruited Hungarian miners who fled to the area as company shareholders. The bridge pictured in the previous chapter was built by Himler Coal Company to transport coal across the Tug River, which cost $450,000 to build at the time. Like many coal mining towns, business was booming, and the communities exploded, becoming lucrative and an ethnic melting pot. In 1922, the Martin Himler mansion was built on a private hilltop, where the man himself lived.

In 1928, massive flooding of the Buck River washed away most of Himlerville, forcing inevitable bankruptcy for the coal company. Martin Himler took this as an omen and moved out of the area to continue his work as a newspaper editor, later serving in the U.S. Army. Pancreatic cancer claimed Martin Himler in 1961, but he did not pass without leaving a massive legacy behind.

After spotting the dilapidated mansion from the road, I parked the car at a local church so I could hike up the mountain. At the time, I had no idea the rich history of this mansion, or that the mansion was listed on the National Register of Historic Places in 1991. On my return, church was in session and my car was blocked in. I apparently got the attention of church ushers, as they looked out the glass doors and knew I didn't belong. One of the men moved the car, but gave me a look that said, "You mean to tell me you used God's house to park and then trespass?" Yes.

The hike up the steep, twisting, overgrown mountain road would have felt like a carnival ride if I were driving. This was the view of the bone-chilling ascent to the mansion, believed by some locals to be haunted.

Once a handcrafted work of art made of stone and concrete has now been taken over by time and natural elements, 100 years later. I will reiterate that walking around random property in Eastern Kentucky isn't always a good idea. This was worth the risk.

Left: This was one of those times when the inside was part of the outside, because there was not much inside, and the toppling made them one.

Below: The fact that the house even stands partially after decades of abandonment speaks well of the original build quality.

Right: Layers of bead board and battered plasterwork on the walls and crumbling remnants of the floors and ceilings are all that remained of the inside.

Below: For years, the Martin County Historical Society has been working on planning a renovation of this historic landmark. I remain skeptical of how this is possible, though I'd be impressed if they accomplished the task. The foundation and brickwork may still be solid. The rest of the house—not so much.

It's safe to say that this wing of the home no longer has an inside. It's all on the ground.

All that remained of the inside was right here. I wonder if Martin Himler would have offered me a drink or pointed a shotgun at me if I came to photograph the house nearly 100 years earlier? I suppose that's a moot point, because if it wasn't abandoned then, even if I were around, I wouldn't have been there.

8

BEYOND BUTCHER HOLLER

I made the transition from Martin County to Johnson County, home of country music star, Loretta Lynn, to explore their backroads. Her song "Coal Miner's Daughter" tells you about life growing up on Butcher Holler, and a lot about the heritage of the coal mining region where she was raised. My two main stops in the area stops both complemented and completely contrasted the other.

It's not uncommon in my travels to see tiny post offices with limited operating hours in small rural communities. However, this is the first abandoned post office I've encountered, tucked away in the tiny community of Nippa. Later in my travels, from the road, I spotted a collection of neglected antique cars and trucks sinking into the field, in the back lot of a rural residential property. The man who lived there was outside, so I took the opportunity to talk to him and photograph the picturesque Detroit relics. Vic, a welder, and I talked for an hour or more about the local area, the decline in area coal mining, and even conspiracy theories. Local experiences like this always complete my adventures when they happen.

Next to a small community fire department sat this forgotten roadside treasure, across marshy overgrown land.

The former post office in Nippa (pronounced "Nippy" by locals) closed in 1985.

Above left: As population declined over the years, the 42136 zip code was done away with and replaced by the Paintsville zip code of 42140.

Above right: I stepped up to the window and no one was there to help me, but that's okay. I helped myself to photos of the retro post office from days gone by.

Post office business has concluded. However, remnants from drifters and an old electric heater are left behind.

This counter once witnessed many exchanges between the clerk and mining families, and plenty of community gossip.

Right: These women's clothes left behind could very well have belonged to the post office clerk.

Below: The mail slot from the outside isn't completely abandoned, as the mice and spiders have since taken residency.

Left: Open weekdays 8:00-2:00, closed Sundays. I couldn't tell if it said anything about Saturdays. It's safe to say that no one is coming back Monday at 8:00 AM.

Below: It's possible that this dilapidated house next to the post office was the residence of the postmaster or clerk.

The floors were extremely bad, and debris covered every inch of floor space, yet I continued. The calendar on the wall was from 2011, more recent than I expected.

I hope I don't fall through the floor. I may dust off the pan, fry some eggs, and make a pot of tea.

Above: These were baseball and wrestling trophies, not usually items left behind, if the occupant survived and relocated. This is a clue.

Left: Adorable or extremely creepy?

I was enjoying a good night's sleep taking in fresh mold, when all of a sudden, a piece of the ceiling falls on me. How inconvenient.

Down the road, I couldn't help but notice this old derelict farmhouse with a rotted foot bridge going across the creek. There were also no roads left to access the property. At one time, there was likely a private road and bridge that started in a family holler.

Vic, the man that owns this property where several antique cars and trucks from yesteryear sat in the field, told me they all belonged to a friend. He was happy to have me take photos and I enjoyed a visit with him. Upon my research, this Willys pickup truck is from 1951-1953.

The texture and patina made this old Willys a fine work of art, though I do hope someone restores it to its former glory.

The Eldorado was Cadillac's first full-size front wheel drive car, this one *circa* 1970.

Another rare find: an International Harvester R-140 truck, from the early to mid-1950s.

The clutch was probably stiff as a brick, and the long throw shifter made you feel like you were driving something of true substance.

This perspective from the road cannot compare to getting up close and personal to what the passersby only sees from the road, if they notice.

9

WOLFE COUNTY BACKROADS

After leaving Johnson County, I traveled west on Mountain Parkway and randomly exited in Wolfe County, with Campton as county seat, to continue my excursion. Located an hour or so from the heart of coal country, the landscape changed in this region of Eastern Kentucky, which provided another exciting contrast to my Eastern Kentucky journeys. The rolling green hills and farmland beautified the backroad scenery in Wolfe County. Those winding roads led me to several rural treasures of yesteryear.

Each region of Eastern Kentucky I visited had its own unique qualities and landscape, as well as industry and history. It's difficult to pick a favorite, as I enjoyed every part of my adventures. Perhaps the most memorable part of my Wolfe County backroad travels: two different farmers drove by on tractors, both waving to each other as we passed by.

Soon after exiting randomly off the Mountain Parkway in Wolfe County to explore the backroads, I discovered what looked like an old-time schoolhouse.

Some one-room schoolhouses had a boy's and girl's outhouse; however, that was perhaps a luxury.

Unfortunately, I was not able to learn any history on this building through community groups or historians. I do, however, think my assessment is correct.

Then there was a randomly placed bed, a paint can, pallets, and a few books. The plot thickens.

Inside was one large empty room, with only one enclosed room, the size of the average bedroom. There was one chimney and a spot where a wood or coal burning stove used to be, all telltale signs of an old-time schoolhouse. Today, the curtains blow in the breeze and the only sounds were my own footsteps.

This old church used to be full of people on Sunday, and I would bet that I was the only visitor that day.

Being slightly west of the heart of coal country, the landscape was different. I enjoyed hilly roads and open meadows, and more of an agricultural vibe than mining. Taking in the ambience was nice, and so was getting inside the church!

Now I can say I preached at a church, if standing in the preacher's spot counts for anything.

It seems that pianos are always left behind in defunct churches, likely due to the difficulty of moving it.

All eyes used to be on this pulpit on Sundays. Maybe Wednesday evenings as well. I wonder if this church participated in snake handling, a ritual in many Appalachian churches. No thank you.

Eastern Kentucky is one of those places where you must be careful before assuming a house is abandoned. Thankfully, this one was.

It never fails that thorn bushes are prevalent when I find these charming old houses.

At one time on this porch, there were rocking chairs and mason jars of sweet iced tea, or possibly a moonshine drink. Now there are warped, rotting boards, broken glass, and vegetation growing over.

Watering the plant now would be pointless. I'm afraid it's too late. The good news: overgrowth is incorporating itself onto the house, if plants are their passion.

The charming rustic utility barn matches the house, and still stands, despite becoming slightly off-kilter with time.

I asked a neighbor what this was. The man told me that it was a root cellar to keep fruits and vegetables, and other foods fresh and cool below ground level. At ground level, shelves stored canned and jarred food, all common practices in the days before refrigeration. The upstairs was used for storage. This building remained, though the house was already razed.

10

THE LAST FISHING TRIP

On the final leg of this tour, in the general direction of home, Breathitt County was my final exploration. The backroads I traveled had sharp hairpin turns, steep hills, and deep valleys with hollers tucked away in places unfathomable to outsiders. In the event of mud or snow, no one gets out of those private roads or driveways tucked in the hills of the mountainous landscape without some sort of four-wheel-drive vehicle.

It takes a seasoned explorer in places like Eastern Kentucky, and many other regions, to have the perfect balance of courage and discretion. Not every place that appears vacant is actually abandoned. One unspoken rule is not to enter the hollers unless someone there knows you. Those are private drives that usually go into a valley, with homes and properties occupied by one or multiple families.

My eye gravitated towards an abandoned house on a hilltop that required entering a holler to access it. I turned the car around to work on a plan of attack. Across the road from that holler, there was a family outside, whose house sat a short distance from the road. I didn't get the feeling that they would be hostile, but they knew it was unusual for the same car to pass by twice, especially at a lower speed. I had their attention, so I decided to satisfy their curiosity and try to gain insider access to the holler.

The matriarch of the family politely but directly asked me what I was looking for. When I explained that I wanted to photograph the abandoned house back in the holler, and told her what I do, she and the rest of the family were intrigued. I learned a bit about the area, had a nice visit with all of them, and got the blessing I needed to explore the old house. I have found Eastern Kentucky people to be kind, hospitable, and eager to share area history. What you see is usually exactly what you get; however, if they see an outsider as a threat, they don't play around.

My new friends told me this old house was built shortly after a major flood in 1939 that claimed many houses in the area.

It was my hope that the house had as much to offer as the front porch did. I was not disappointed.

Right: The first discovery upon entry was an old fishing pole in the mudroom/foyer. This random find has a more emotional impact after learning that the elderly widower and grandfather who lived in the house had passed away several years before this point. My first thought was that I hoped he got to make that one last fishing trip.

Below: I thought I told you to stop putting your old mason jars on top of the air hockey table, and to get rid of that old wallpaper! I'm sorry, maybe tomorrow, or the tomorrow after that. Here we are.

I don't know whether to appreciate this old antique sofa with the flowery pattern or say it's hideous. Maybe both.

Most of the furnishings and knick-knacks look relatively undisturbed, probably because strangers won't usually lurk in the hollers.

Grandpa's old bedroom looks relatively unruffled. Even the 1960s suitcase still remains. Time has accelerated the decline of the old house since his departure.

With cleaning, these classic vinyl LPs probably still play nicely. These are original albums from the mid-to-late 1960s (Johnny Cash) and very early 1970s (Conway Twitty).

The fires have burned recently, despite the house being officially unoccupied. It's also a bit eerie to see family photos and heirlooms left behind. They always tell a story.

11

LEARNING IN LYNCH

The town of Lynch, Kentucky, was built and established in 1917 by the U.S. Coal And Coke Company, a subsidiary of U.S. Steel. The company built homes for the miners and their families, made up of six coal camps within Lynch. Like many coal companies, the company also established churches, parks, medical facilities, a large company store, a post office, schools, and more for its resident mining families. A 108-room hotel was built to provide living accommodations for hospital staff, coal mine officials and engineers, and store employees. A theater, restaurant, and retail shops were among some of the hotel amenities.

U.S. Steel closely modeled Lynch after their Gary, West Virginia, coal camp. The community, and business was booming. Immigrants from almost forty different countries arriving at Ellis Island set foot on U.S. soil seeking opportunities, and were recruited by U.S. Steel. In the pinnacle of the coal mining days in Lynch, the population reached around 10,000 and was a melting pot that many mining families were proud to call home.

By the early 1960s, the mines being nearly empty, and the introduction of more mechanized methods of coal mining caused many employees to be laid off. Subsequently, those workers and their families had to leave Lynch, since they lived in company housing, and sought opportunities elsewhere.

A Lynch native and historian was kind enough to provide a wealth of historical and insider information. He recalls that in the mid-1960s, the racially segregated school system was integrated sooner than most in surrounding areas were. Families of different ethnicities and races grew accustomed to associating with one another, and their children played together in the parks and streets. These breakthroughs in oppressive times, and the overall sense of community, are fondly remembered by the native generation of its coal mining families.

In 1984, when U.S. Steel sold their operation and fled Lynch, the population continued to dwindle. In 2020, when my friend, Jerry Winnett, and I visited the charming, proud, tightly-knit community trying to keep it together, the population was below 800 people.

Above: This is the original site of the Lynch Colored Public School, built in 1923. The building is used by the Eastern Kentucky Social Club, who built the memorial to honor black coal miners. The painted bicycles planted across the community are to celebrate the new greenways and bring a progressive movement to the town.

Left: The school system desegregated in 1963. For years after, this school then served as a middle school, for grades 7 and 8.

I first saw the old Lynch High School and thought, "Where have you been all my life?" The side entrance is pictured here. As usual, the goal was to get inside before focusing on the street view.

The back of the school was choked by overgrowth, though the fine workmanship was still plenty visible. The school was built in 1924 with native sandstone from Black Mountain, by Italian stone masons working for U.S. Steel.

The stunning interior was mostly intact, though ravaged by vandalism and the effects of time. The stairs were heavily packed with dirt and building debris, making footing a bit unsteady.

These are some old school lockers with a combination lock.

The retro colors are on full display in the old lunchroom.

Above: These were my clues that helped me identify this space as a lunchroom.

Left: A look outside the window at the back of the school made me think about the asylum in *Abandoned Alabama: Dark Shadows Of Generations Past.* Especially when seeing that eerie steel staircase.

I can picture being sat here for detention and this being my view. Not everyone would find this view as perfect as I do.

After making our way into the gymnasium, I wondered what pyromaniac was hanging out there before.

Above: These were once the bleachers where spectators would watch basketball games, which is the sport Kentucky is known for.

Left: Even with the divider in place, this could have been an awkward setting in the school locker room.

The wide view of the gymnasium will show how bad the original wood floor has deteriorated with time.

These hallways were every bit as haunting as the inside of the asylum. Mix the darkness with narrow paths of light, debris, deterioration, and the sound of water dripping from the ceiling.

I was trapped in the dampness, cold, and darkness. Only this window shines light into that darkness, though that doesn't mean I want to leave.

Sorry, I'm late for class. Decades late. Sorry.

I will never forget a trick I leaned in school to prank the teachers. Place the pieces of chalk between the slats of the eraser, and the teacher is simultaneously scribbling on the blackboard while erasing. Once they hear the sound, they usually want a word with the person who did it.

I've always loved texture and the lead paint chipping off. This classroom has so much character.

The brick ruins, I believe, were an add-on wing used for home economics and other elective classes.

This old metal mop bucket wringer is an antique, as they've been made out of plastic for as long as I remember.

It was a chilly and windy day, perfect for exploring. The icicles hanging from the leaking ceiling give you an added sensory detail of our exploration.

Walking through this when it all fell would have been someone's bad luck.

The upstairs level housed most of the classrooms.

I kept seeing those evil looking rototiller-like tines, thinking people were in there chopping up bodies, then I realized they were light fixture deflectors. So much for imagination.

The view down the staircase.

Now we finally made our way to the street side view. My angles were limited because neighbors park their cars in front of it if they run out of driveway. I felt the building was more interesting than their cars.

This was the first time we got to see the opposite side of the old Lynch High School, and by then, we discovered another building next to it!

Right: The final graduating class of Lynch High School was in 1981 due to the lack of students in the area. When the Lynch schools closed, students were sent to Benham and Cumberland.

Below: The Lynch Graded And High School was built *circa* 1920. It was soon outgrown, then made a grade school, while next door the high school was built. As you can see, the design and architecture were the same.

Two of my favorite things: garbage, and an invitation inside.

I saw vines and trees growing on the rooftops and inside the classrooms, yet the building remains upright. The floors upstairs were weak in parts, but it was worth the risk.

You thought I was joking?

With the old desks, rotted TV cabinet, and the sheer destruction surrounding them, this is the closest I've been to Chernobyl. For now.

Once a nurturing learning environment, it now suffers in the aftermath of nearly forty years of abandonment.

All it takes is an airborne seed, dirt, water, and sun, and a sapling is born.

Generations of students sat and studied at this desk, now rusted remains are its voice once again.

It's slightly disconcerting not being able to see the floor, although it was strong enough to hold all the earth washed in and other items left behind.

The school grounds between the grade school and the high school was once nicely manicured. Now, even from the window, you can see where vegetation has taken over.

No abandoned mission is ever complete without bad graffiti and a mattress or two.

Despite the lovely stonework, there was no need to go far in this room, due to a giant hole in the floor towards the corner of the room.

Narrow hallways are usually the creepiest, though this smaller school had a greater space/window ratio and not as much flashlight use was necessary to navigate. I hope you've enjoyed this special excursion.

12

THE COMPANY STORE

The Mary Helen Coal Company began mine operations and built their company town in Coalgood, Kentucky, in 1919. Jerry and I had the pleasure of exploring the badly distressed Mary Helen Commissary, the only remaining company structure besides the church that still operated and the old adjacent livestock feed house. The company store was where its workers purchased their food, household goods, clothing, etc., and paid for it in company scrip (which was part of their wages besides money).

I spoke with community native, Mr. Brad Sears, to learn the history of Mary Helen and the commissary building. Brad grew up in the community while his parents, William H. and Aretta Sears, were longtime company employees. The original Mary Helen company store was a smaller wooden building, eventually replaced with this much larger three-story brick building in the 1930s. The company store was not only the lifeline for the community's supplies, but an important hub of the community where the families would gather, even off the clock.

Circa 1960, Mary Helen Coal Company sold the mine to the Sigmon brothers. As more mechanization took place, a considerable amount of jobs were cut. The store remained open, though it was no longer a company store. Dorthy Shepherd and butcher, Lee Haynes, took over the store, becoming S & H Store. Mrs. Sears worked at the store, and eventually took over operations when Mr. Haynes fell ill. She also worked the grill and post office, spending most of her working years at the emporium.

The lower level housed The Grill (the name of the small eatery), a barber shop, and a doctor's office. The second level was the store/butcher shop that sold everything local families needed, the mine safety and payroll office, and the community post office. The third level was where the company store once sold furniture. The Grill closed *circa* 1990, with the store soon following suit. Mr. and Mrs. Sears lived in the last remaining company house until the early 1990s. The post office was the last to operate in the building, closing in 2004.

The second-level entrance, where the green brick is, was the main commissary entrance. Below it was The Grill. Off to the side was the post office, mine office, doctor's office, and the barbershop.

This was the ground floor entrance to the post office. Walk up the steps and you were there. Brad Sears remembers the lady running the post office raising the American flag up the pole every morning, and lowering it when closing for the day.

The only remaining items in The Grill were the wooden booths, an old coffee pot, building debris, and some restaurant inspection records from 1988. Its closure was inevitable soon after when it could no longer compete with fast food chains opening in Harlan.

Brad recalls a painted glass sign in green letters, "The Grill," an ice cream cooler, pop machines, and glass cases with candy, tobacco products, and more goodies.

Left: Thankfully, in this part of The Grill, that thick muddy mess was mostly dried up. By the entrance, it was still wet and an inch of it stuck to my shoes. I did discover a nice tile floor underneath the formation. I still haven't decided if the mud-like substance was from washed earth and flooding, or coal slurry that crept into the lower level.

Below: It was time to visit the company store, thankfully not owing my soul to it. Goods were brought to the store by train and delivery trucks.

The bare shelves, pressed tin ceiling, textured brickwork, and a walk-in cooler are all that remained. Perhaps the miners of bygone eras spirits were watching me. I will take that as an opportunity to tell what may be the final story of this commissary to the best of my ability.

Now silent and cold, these steam radiators are slowly being swallowed by obsolescence and father time.

Once loaded with merchandise and patrons, now idle bare shelves indicate goods are indefinitely out of stock.

Neighborhood children were always welcome to warm up in the store in the winter, and come inside to grab a pop or ice cream while outside playing in the summertime. In his boyhood, Brad was given some small odd jobs around the store which provided him with some spending money.

This was a post office window from inside the store. The boarded-up window was likely used to access the payroll office before the post office moved into the commissary building, *circa* 1960.

The vintage hardwood floor was surprisingly solid, until approaching this back corner of the building.

The lonely squeak the doors make pales in comparison to the heavy traffic from several generations that used to pass through.

I walked around the upper level porch to access the post office, and in the old lobby were boxes, several decades old, containing records and part of an old two-wheel dolly.

The two rooms down the hall on the second level were used as the coal mine safety office and payroll office/ record keeping. The roof and floors in this part of the building were weaker, so I proceeded with some caution.

These boxes of records dated from 1990-1993 for Bell and Harlan Counties. This was the farthest back room in the building, which was the weakest part throughout.

The patterned glass facing the hallway on the office doors and windows had a retro charm, though was not the industrial steel reinforced glass seen in factories.

The split door allowed postal workers to access the business end of the post office, while creating a barrier to keep unauthorized personnel out.

I did not expect to find this classic Diebold safe left behind! It was dated 1955 and was loaded with papers.

Cleanliness is godliness. Speaking of cleanliness, there used to be a bath house across the road where miners showered after their shift. In the early days of mining, many homes still did not have indoor showers.

Left: Generations of mine workers and their families passed through this door, conducting business and engaging in plenty of friendly community banter. Part of its rare character is the afterhours mail slot in the center of the door, where outgoing mail waited for the morning clerk in a collection tray.

Below: At this back corner of the building, facing the train tracks, Brad recalls an inside freight elevator used to lift furniture to the upper level. Also, in this vicinity, there was a tank with a manual pump that dispensed coal oil sold by the store. Across the tracks was the feed house. The inside area of this wing was also used for storage.

Though mining activity isn't what it was in the Mary Helen glory days, the mine remains active, having changed hands several times since. The day was perfect to explore with brisk air, rushing high waters, and misty mountaintops.

The rich history and the stories these walls could tell makes this adventure almost beyond compare. I was able to walk through all the building, except maybe this part.

This errant tree sure is wreaking havoc on the building, perhaps seeking revenge for any trees that were cleared while building the empire.

The Mary Helen United Methodist Church was still operational. This elevated walking bridge allows churchgoers to cross the railroad tracks, in the event of a unit train blocking the road and church access. I hope you've enjoyed my Eastern Kentucky adventures.

MORE BY JAY FARRELL

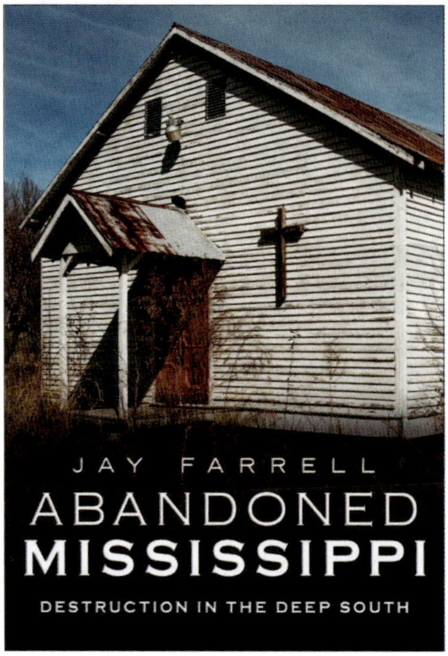

ABANDONED MISSISSIPPI

ISBN: 978-1-63499-179-7

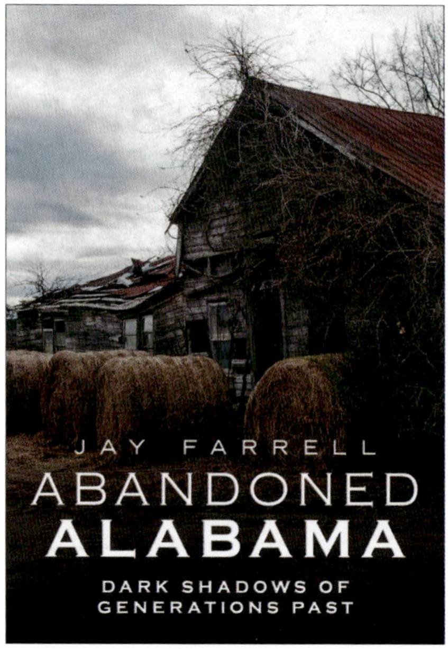

ABANDONED ALABAMA
VOLUME 2

ISBN: 978-1-63499-161-2

ABANDONED NASHVILLE

ISBN: 978-1-63499-113-1

ABANDONED TENNESSEE
VOLUME 1

ISBN: 978-1-63499-055-4